This Scripture Journal belongs to

_____

# SCRIPTURE JOURNAL

*Topics Studied:*

|  | *Sunday* | *Monday* | *Tuesday* |
|---|---|---|---|
| Come Follow Me | | | |
| Book of Mormon | | | |
| Searching: *Connections* *Patterns* *Themes* | | | |

*Insights, Experiences, Revelations*

_____
_____
_____
_____
_____
_____
_____
_____
_____
_____
_____
_____
_____
_____
_____
_____
_____
_____

WEEK OF  TO

| Wednesday | Thursday | Friday | Saturday |
|---|---|---|---|
| | | | |
| | | | |
| | | | |

# SCRIPTURE JOURNAL

*Topics Studied:*

|  | *Sunday* | *Monday* | *Tuesday* |
|---|---|---|---|
| **Come Follow Me** | | | |
| **Book of Mormon** | | | |
| **Searching:** *Connections* *Patterns* *Themes* | | | |

*Insights, Experiences, Revelations*

_____
_____
_____
_____
_____
_____
_____
_____
_____
_____
_____
_____
_____
_____
_____
_____
_____
_____

WEEK OF　　　　　　　　　　　TO

| Wednesday | Thursday | Friday | Saturday |
|---|---|---|---|
|  |  |  |  |
|  |  |  |  |
|  |  |  |  |

# SCRIPTURE JOURNAL

*Topics Studied:*

|  | *Sunday* | *Monday* | *Tuesday* |
|---|---|---|---|
| Come Follow Me |  |  |  |
| Book of Mormon |  |  |  |
| Searching: *Connections* *Patterns* *Themes* |  |  |  |

*Insights, Experiences, Revelations*

_____
_____
_____
_____
_____
_____
_____
_____
_____
_____
_____
_____
_____
_____
_____
_____
_____
_____
_____

WEEK OF                                    TO

| Wednesday | Thursday | Friday | Saturday |
|-----------|----------|--------|----------|
|           |          |        |          |
|           |          |        |          |
|           |          |        |          |

_____
_____
_____
_____
_____
_____
_____
_____
_____
_____
_____
_____
_____
_____
_____
_____
_____
_____
_____

# SCRIPTURE JOURNAL

*Topics Studied:*

|  | *Sunday* | *Monday* | *Tuesday* |
|---|---|---|---|
| **Come Follow Me** | | | |
| **Book of Mormon** | | | |
| **Searching:** *Connections* *Patterns* *Themes* | | | |

*Insights, Experiences, Revelations*

_____
_____
_____
_____
_____
_____
_____
_____
_____
_____
_____
_____
_____
_____
_____
_____
_____

WEEK OF                              TO

| Wednesday | Thursday | Friday | Saturday |
|---|---|---|---|
|  |  |  |  |
|  |  |  |  |
|  |  |  |  |

_____
_____
_____
_____
_____
_____
_____
_____
_____
_____
_____
_____
_____
_____
_____
_____
_____
_____

# SCRIPTURE JOURNAL

*Topics Studied:*

|  | *Sunday* | *Monday* | *Tuesday* |
|---|---|---|---|
| Come Follow Me | | | |
| Book of Mormon | | | |
| Searching: *Connections*  *Patterns*  *Themes* | | | |

*Insights, Experiences, Revelations*

_____
_____
_____
_____
_____
_____
_____
_____
_____
_____
_____
_____
_____
_____
_____
_____
_____
_____
_____

WEEK OF                                    TO

| Wednesday | Thursday | Friday | Saturday |
|---|---|---|---|
|  |  |  |  |
|  |  |  |  |
|  |  |  |  |

# SCRIPTURE JOURNAL

*Topics Studied:*

|  | *Sunday* | *Monday* | *Tuesday* |
|---|---|---|---|
| Come Follow Me |  |  |  |
| Book of Mormon |  |  |  |
| Searching: *Connections* *Patterns* *Themes* |  |  |  |

*Insights, Experiences, Revelations*

_____
_____
_____
_____
_____
_____
_____
_____
_____
_____
_____
_____
_____
_____
_____
_____
_____
_____
_____

WEEK OF				TO

| Wednesday | Thursday | Friday | Saturday |
|---|---|---|---|
|  |  |  |  |
|  |  |  |  |
|  |  |  |  |

# SCRIPTURE JOURNAL

*Topics Studied:*

|  | *Sunday* | *Monday* | *Tuesday* |
|---|---|---|---|
| Come Follow Me | | | |
| Book of Mormon | | | |
| Searching: *Connections* *Patterns* *Themes* | | | |

*Insights, Experiences, Revelations*

_____
_____
_____
_____
_____
_____
_____
_____
_____
_____
_____
_____
_____
_____
_____
_____
_____

WEEK OF                              TO

| Wednesday | Thursday | Friday | Saturday |
|---|---|---|---|
|  |  |  |  |
|  |  |  |  |
|  |  |  |  |

_____
_____
_____
_____
_____
_____
_____
_____
_____
_____
_____
_____
_____
_____
_____
_____
_____
_____

# SCRIPTURE JOURNAL

*Topics Studied:*

|  | *Sunday* | *Monday* | *Tuesday* |
|---|---|---|---|
| **Come Follow Me** | | | |
| **Book of Mormon** | | | |
| **Searching:** *Connections* *Patterns* *Themes* | | | |

*Insights, Experiences, Revelations*

_____
_____
_____
_____
_____
_____
_____
_____
_____
_____
_____
_____
_____
_____
_____
_____
_____
_____

WEEK OF     TO

| Wednesday | Thursday | Friday | Saturday |
|---|---|---|---|
|  |  |  |  |
|  |  |  |  |
|  |  |  |  |

# SCRIPTURE JOURNAL

*Topics Studied:*

|  | *Sunday* | *Monday* | *Tuesday* |
|---|---|---|---|
| Come Follow Me | | | |
| Book of Mormon | | | |
| Searching: *Connections*  *Patterns*  *Themes* | | | |

*Insights, Experiences, Revelations*

_____
_____
_____
_____
_____
_____
_____
_____
_____
_____
_____
_____
_____
_____
_____
_____
_____
_____
_____

WEEK OF						TO

| Wednesday | Thursday | Friday | Saturday |
|---|---|---|---|
|  |  |  |  |
|  |  |  |  |
|  |  |  |  |

# SCRIPTURE JOURNAL

*Topics Studied:*

|  | *Sunday* | *Monday* | *Tuesday* |
|---|---|---|---|
| **Come Follow Me** | | | |
| **Book of Mormon** | | | |
| **Searching:** *Connections* *Patterns* *Themes* | | | |

*Insights, Experiences, Revelations*

_____
_____
_____
_____
_____
_____
_____
_____
_____
_____
_____
_____
_____
_____
_____
_____
_____
_____

WEEK OF                                    TO

| Wednesday | Thursday | Friday | Saturday |
|---|---|---|---|
|  |  |  |  |
|  |  |  |  |
|  |  |  |  |

# SCRIPTURE JOURNAL

*Topics Studied:*

|  | *Sunday* | *Monday* | *Tuesday* |
|---|---|---|---|
| Come Follow Me | | | |
| Book of Mormon | | | |
| Searching: *Connections* *Patterns* *Themes* | | | |

*Insights, Experiences, Revelations*

_____
_____
_____
_____
_____
_____
_____
_____
_____
_____
_____
_____
_____
_____
_____
_____
_____
_____
_____

WEEK OF                              TO

| Wednesday | Thursday | Friday | Saturday |
|-----------|----------|--------|----------|
|           |          |        |          |
|           |          |        |          |
|           |          |        |          |

___
___
___
___
___
___
___
___
___
___
___
___
___
___
___
___
___
___

# SCRIPTURE JOURNAL

*Topics Studied:*

|  | *Sunday* | *Monday* | *Tuesday* |
|---|---|---|---|
| **Come Follow Me** | | | |
| **Book of Mormon** | | | |
| **Searching:** *Connections* *Patterns* *Themes* | | | |

*Insights, Experiences, Revelations*

_____
_____
_____
_____
_____
_____
_____
_____
_____
_____
_____
_____
_____
_____
_____
_____
_____
_____

WEEK OF                              TO

| Wednesday | Thursday | Friday | Saturday |
|---|---|---|---|
|  |  |  |  |
|  |  |  |  |
|  |  |  |  |

# SCRIPTURE JOURNAL

*Topics Studied:*

|  | *Sunday* | *Monday* | *Tuesday* |
|---|---|---|---|
| Come Follow Me | | | |
| Book of Mormon | | | |
| Searching: *Connections*  *Patterns*  *Themes* | | | |

*Insights, Experiences, Revelations*

_____
_____
_____
_____
_____
_____
_____
_____
_____
_____
_____
_____
_____
_____
_____
_____
_____
_____

WEEK OF                              TO

| Wednesday | Thursday | Friday | Saturday |
|-----------|----------|--------|----------|
|           |          |        |          |
|           |          |        |          |
|           |          |        |          |

_____
_____
_____
_____
_____
_____
_____
_____
_____
_____
_____
_____
_____
_____
_____
_____
_____

# SCRIPTURE JOURNAL

*Topics Studied:*

|  | Sunday | Monday | Tuesday |
|---|---|---|---|
| **Come Follow Me** | | | |
| **Book of Mormon** | | | |
| **Searching:** *Connections*  *Patterns*  *Themes* | | | |

*Insights, Experiences, Revelations*

_____
_____
_____
_____
_____
_____
_____
_____
_____
_____
_____
_____
_____
_____
_____
_____
_____
_____

WEEK OF                              TO

| Wednesday | Thursday | Friday | Saturday |
|-----------|----------|--------|----------|
|           |          |        |          |
|           |          |        |          |
|           |          |        |          |

_____
_____
_____
_____
_____
_____
_____
_____
_____
_____
_____
_____
_____
_____
_____
_____
_____

# SCRIPTURE JOURNAL

*Topics Studied:*

|  | *Sunday* | *Monday* | *Tuesday* |
|---|---|---|---|
| Come Follow Me | | | |
| Book of Mormon | | | |
| Searching: *Connections* *Patterns* *Themes* | | | |

*Insights, Experiences, Revelations*

_____
_____
_____
_____
_____
_____
_____
_____
_____
_____
_____
_____
_____
_____
_____
_____
_____
_____

WEEK OF                              TO

| Wednesday | Thursday | Friday | Saturday |
|---|---|---|---|
|  |  |  |  |
|  |  |  |  |
|  |  |  |  |

_____
_____
_____
_____
_____
_____
_____
_____
_____
_____
_____
_____
_____
_____
_____
_____

# SCRIPTURE JOURNAL

*Topics Studied:*

|  | *Sunday* | *Monday* | *Tuesday* |
|---|---|---|---|
| Come Follow Me | | | |
| Book of Mormon | | | |
| Searching: *Connections* *Patterns* *Themes* | | | |

*Insights, Experiences, Revelations*

_____
_____
_____
_____
_____
_____
_____
_____
_____
_____
_____
_____
_____
_____
_____
_____
_____
_____

WEEK OF                           TO

| Wednesday | Thursday | Friday | Saturday |
|-----------|----------|--------|----------|
|           |          |        |          |
|           |          |        |          |
|           |          |        |          |

# SCRIPTURE JOURNAL

*Topics Studied:*

|  | *Sunday* | *Monday* | *Tuesday* |
|---|---|---|---|
| Come Follow Me | | | |
| Book of Mormon | | | |
| Searching: *Connections* *Patterns* *Themes* | | | |

*Insights, Experiences, Revelations*

_____
_____
_____
_____
_____
_____
_____
_____
_____
_____
_____
_____
_____
_____
_____
_____
_____
_____

WEEK OF                                TO

| Wednesday | Thursday | Friday | Saturday |
|---|---|---|---|
|  |  |  |  |
|  |  |  |  |
|  |  |  |  |

_____
_____
_____
_____
_____
_____
_____
_____
_____
_____
_____
_____
_____
_____
_____
_____
_____

# SCRIPTURE JOURNAL

*Topics Studied:*

|  | *Sunday* | *Monday* | *Tuesday* |
|---|---|---|---|
| Come Follow Me | | | |
| Book of Mormon | | | |
| Searching: *Connections* *Patterns* *Themes* | | | |

*Insights, Experiences, Revelations*

_____
_____
_____
_____
_____
_____
_____
_____
_____
_____
_____
_____
_____
_____
_____
_____
_____
_____

WEEK OF                                    TO

| Wednesday | Thursday | Friday | Saturday |
|-----------|----------|--------|----------|
|           |          |        |          |
|           |          |        |          |
|           |          |        |          |

# SCRIPTURE JOURNAL

*Topics Studied:*

|  | *Sunday* | *Monday* | *Tuesday* |
|---|---|---|---|
| Come Follow Me | | | |
| Book of Mormon | | | |
| Searching: *Connections* *Patterns* *Themes* | | | |

*Insights, Experiences, Revelations*

_____
_____
_____
_____
_____
_____
_____
_____
_____
_____
_____
_____
_____
_____
_____
_____
_____
_____

WEEK OF                                TO

| Wednesday | Thursday | Friday | Saturday |
|-----------|----------|--------|----------|
|           |          |        |          |
|           |          |        |          |
|           |          |        |          |

# SCRIPTURE JOURNAL

*Topics Studied:*

|  | *Sunday* | *Monday* | *Tuesday* |
|---|---|---|---|
| **Come Follow Me** | | | |
| **Book of Mormon** | | | |
| **Searching:** *Connections* *Patterns* *Themes* | | | |

*Insights, Experiences, Revelations*

_____
_____
_____
_____
_____
_____
_____
_____
_____
_____
_____
_____
_____
_____
_____
_____
_____
_____

WEEK OF                              TO

| Wednesday | Thursday | Friday | Saturday |
|-----------|----------|--------|----------|
|           |          |        |          |
|           |          |        |          |
|           |          |        |          |

_____
_____
_____
_____
_____
_____
_____
_____
_____
_____
_____
_____
_____
_____
_____
_____
_____

# SCRIPTURE JOURNAL

*Topics Studied:*

|  | *Sunday* | *Monday* | *Tuesday* |
|---|---|---|---|
| Come Follow Me | | | |
| Book of Mormon | | | |
| Searching: *Connections*  *Patterns*  *Themes* | | | |

*Insights, Experiences, Revelations*

_____
_____
_____
_____
_____
_____
_____
_____
_____
_____
_____
_____
_____
_____
_____
_____
_____
_____
_____

WEEK OF                           TO

| Wednesday | Thursday | Friday | Saturday |
|-----------|----------|--------|----------|
|           |          |        |          |
|           |          |        |          |
|           |          |        |          |

_____
_____
_____
_____
_____
_____
_____
_____
_____
_____
_____
_____
_____
_____
_____
_____

# SCRIPTURE JOURNAL

*Topics Studied:*

|  | *Sunday* | *Monday* | *Tuesday* |
|---|---|---|---|
| **Come Follow Me** |  |  |  |
| **Book of Mormon** |  |  |  |
| **Searching:** *Connections* *Patterns* *Themes* |  |  |  |

*Insights, Experiences, Revelations*

_____
_____
_____
_____
_____
_____
_____
_____
_____
_____
_____
_____
_____
_____
_____
_____
_____

WEEK OF                                TO

| Wednesday | Thursday | Friday | Saturday |
|---|---|---|---|
|  |  |  |  |
|  |  |  |  |
|  |  |  |  |

_____
_____
_____
_____
_____
_____
_____
_____
_____
_____
_____
_____
_____
_____
_____
_____
_____

# SCRIPTURE JOURNAL

*Topics Studied:*

|  | *Sunday* | *Monday* | *Tuesday* |
|---|---|---|---|
| **Come Follow Me** | | | |
| **Book of Mormon** | | | |
| **Searching:** *Connections* *Patterns* *Themes* | | | |

*Insights, Experiences, Revelations*

_____
_____
_____
_____
_____
_____
_____
_____
_____
_____
_____
_____
_____
_____
_____
_____
_____

WEEK OF                              TO

| Wednesday | Thursday | Friday | Saturday |
|---|---|---|---|
|  |  |  |  |
|  |  |  |  |
|  |  |  |  |

_____
_____
_____
_____
_____
_____
_____
_____
_____
_____
_____
_____
_____
_____
_____

# SCRIPTURE JOURNAL

*Topics Studied:*

|  | Sunday | Monday | Tuesday |
|---|---|---|---|
| **Come Follow Me** | | | |
| **Book of Mormon** | | | |
| **Searching:** *Connections* *Patterns* *Themes* | | | |

*Insights, Experiences, Revelations*

_____
_____
_____
_____
_____
_____
_____
_____
_____
_____
_____
_____
_____
_____
_____
_____
_____
_____

WEEK OF						TO

| Wednesday | Thursday | Friday | Saturday |
|---|---|---|---|
|  |  |  |  |
|  |  |  |  |
|  |  |  |  |

# SCRIPTURE JOURNAL

*Topics Studied:*

|  | *Sunday* | *Monday* | *Tuesday* |
|---|---|---|---|
| Come Follow Me | | | |
| Book of Mormon | | | |
| Searching: *Connections* *Patterns* *Themes* | | | |

*Insights, Experiences, Revelations*

_____
_____
_____
_____
_____
_____
_____
_____
_____
_____
_____
_____
_____
_____
_____
_____
_____

WEEK OF                              TO

| Wednesday | Thursday | Friday | Saturday |
|---|---|---|---|
|  |  |  |  |
|  |  |  |  |
|  |  |  |  |

_____
_____
_____
_____
_____
_____
_____
_____
_____
_____
_____
_____
_____
_____
_____
_____
_____
_____
―

# SCRIPTURE JOURNAL

*Topics Studied:*

|  | Sunday | Monday | Tuesday |
|---|---|---|---|
| **Come Follow Me** | | | |
| **Book of Mormon** | | | |
| **Searching:** *Connections* <br><br> *Patterns* <br><br> *Themes* | | | |

*Insights, Experiences, Revelations*

_____
_____
_____
_____
_____
_____
_____
_____
_____
_____
_____
_____
_____
_____
_____
_____
_____
_____

WEEK OF	TO

| Wednesday | Thursday | Friday | Saturday |
|---|---|---|---|
|  |  |  |  |
|  |  |  |  |
|  |  |  |  |

# SCRIPTURE JOURNAL

*Topics Studied:*

|  | *Sunday* | *Monday* | *Tuesday* |
|---|---|---|---|
| Come Follow Me | | | |
| Book of Mormon | | | |
| Searching: *Connections*  *Patterns*  *Themes* | | | |

*Insights, Experiences, Revelations*

_____
_____
_____
_____
_____
_____
_____
_____
_____
_____
_____
_____
_____
_____
_____
_____
_____

WEEK OF                              TO

| Wednesday | Thursday | Friday | Saturday |
|---|---|---|---|
|  |  |  |  |
|  |  |  |  |
|  |  |  |  |

_____
_____
_____
_____
_____
_____
_____
_____
_____
_____
_____
_____
_____
_____
_____
_____
_____

# SCRIPTURE JOURNAL

*Topics Studied:*

|  | Sunday | Monday | Tuesday |
|---|---|---|---|
| **Come Follow Me** | | | |
| **Book of Mormon** | | | |
| **Searching:** *Connections* *Patterns* *Themes* | | | |

*Insights, Experiences, Revelations*

_____
_____
_____
_____
_____
_____
_____
_____
_____
_____
_____
_____
_____
_____
_____
_____
_____
_____

WEEK OF                              TO

| Wednesday | Thursday | Friday | Saturday |
|-----------|----------|--------|----------|
|           |          |        |          |
|           |          |        |          |
|           |          |        |          |

_____
_____
_____
_____
_____
_____
_____
_____
_____
_____
_____
_____
_____
_____
_____
_____
_____

# SCRIPTURE JOURNAL

*Topics Studied:*

|  | *Sunday* | *Monday* | *Tuesday* |
|---|---|---|---|
| Come Follow Me | | | |
| Book of Mormon | | | |
| Searching: *Connections* *Patterns* *Themes* | | | |

*Insights, Experiences, Revelations*

_____
_____
_____
_____
_____
_____
_____
_____
_____
_____
_____
_____
_____
_____
_____
_____
_____

WEEK OF                              TO

| Wednesday | Thursday | Friday | Saturday |
|-----------|----------|--------|----------|
|           |          |        |          |
|           |          |        |          |
|           |          |        |          |

_____
_____
_____
_____
_____
_____
_____
_____
_____
_____
_____
_____
_____
_____
_____
_____
_____

# SCRIPTURE JOURNAL

*Topics Studied:*

|  | Sunday | Monday | Tuesday |
|---|---|---|---|
| **Come Follow Me** | | | |
| **Book of Mormon** | | | |
| **Searching:** *Connections* *Patterns* *Themes* | | | |

*Insights, Experiences, Revelations*

_____
_____
_____
_____
_____
_____
_____
_____
_____
_____
_____
_____
_____
_____
_____
_____
_____
_____
_____

WEEK OF                                    TO

| Wednesday | Thursday | Friday | Saturday |
|-----------|----------|--------|----------|
|           |          |        |          |
|           |          |        |          |
|           |          |        |          |

# SCRIPTURE JOURNAL

*Topics Studied:*

|  | *Sunday* | *Monday* | *Tuesday* |
|---|---|---|---|
| Come Follow Me | | | |
| Book of Mormon | | | |
| Searching: *Connections* *Patterns* *Themes* | | | |

*Insights, Experiences, Revelations*

_____
_____
_____
_____
_____
_____
_____
_____
_____
_____
_____
_____
_____
_____
_____
_____

WEEK OF                                   TO

| Wednesday | Thursday | Friday | Saturday |
|-----------|----------|--------|----------|
|           |          |        |          |
|           |          |        |          |
|           |          |        |          |

_____
_____
_____
_____
_____
_____
_____
_____
_____
_____
_____
_____
_____
_____
_____
_____
_____

# SCRIPTURE JOURNAL

*Topics Studied:*

|  | Sunday | Monday | Tuesday |
|---|---|---|---|
| Come Follow Me | | | |
| Book of Mormon | | | |
| Searching: *Connections* *Patterns* *Themes* | | | |

*Insights, Experiences, Revelations*

_____
_____
_____
_____
_____
_____
_____
_____
_____
_____
_____
_____
_____
_____
_____
_____
_____
_____
_____

WEEK OF                                    TO

| Wednesday | Thursday | Friday | Saturday |
|---|---|---|---|
|  |  |  |  |
|  |  |  |  |
|  |  |  |  |

_____
_____
_____
_____
_____
_____
_____
_____
_____
_____
_____
_____
_____
_____
_____
_____

# SCRIPTURE JOURNAL

*Topics Studied:*

|  | *Sunday* | *Monday* | *Tuesday* |
|---|---|---|---|
| Come Follow Me | | | |
| Book of Mormon | | | |
| Searching: *Connections* *Patterns* *Themes* | | | |

*Insights, Experiences, Revelations*

_____
_____
_____
_____
_____
_____
_____
_____
_____
_____
_____
_____
_____
_____
_____
_____
_____

WEEK OF                              TO

| Wednesday | Thursday | Friday | Saturday |
|---|---|---|---|
|  |  |  |  |
|  |  |  |  |
|  |  |  |  |

_____
_____
_____
_____
_____
_____
_____
_____
_____
_____
_____
_____
_____
_____
_____
_____
_____

# SCRIPTURE JOURNAL

*Topics Studied:*

|  | Sunday | Monday | Tuesday |
|---|---|---|---|
| Come Follow Me | | | |
| Book of Mormon | | | |
| Searching: *Connections* *Patterns* *Themes* | | | |

*Insights, Experiences, Revelations*

_____
_____
_____
_____
_____
_____
_____
_____
_____
_____
_____
_____
_____
_____
_____
_____
_____
_____

WEEK OF	TO

| Wednesday | Thursday | Friday | Saturday |
|---|---|---|---|
|  |  |  |  |
|  |  |  |  |
|  |  |  |  |

# SCRIPTURE JOURNAL

*Topics Studied:*

|  | *Sunday* | *Monday* | *Tuesday* |
|---|---|---|---|
| **Come Follow Me** | | | |
| **Book of Mormon** | | | |
| **Searching:** *Connections* *Patterns* *Themes* | | | |

*Insights, Experiences, Revelations*

_____
_____
_____
_____
_____
_____
_____
_____
_____
_____
_____
_____
_____
_____
_____
_____
_____

WEEK OF                                    TO

| Wednesday | Thursday | Friday | Saturday |
|-----------|----------|--------|----------|
|           |          |        |          |
|           |          |        |          |
|           |          |        |          |

_____
_____
_____
_____
_____
_____
_____
_____
_____
_____
_____
_____
_____
_____
_____
_____

# SCRIPTURE JOURNAL

*Topics Studied:*

|  | Sunday | Monday | Tuesday |
|---|---|---|---|
| **Come Follow Me** | | | |
| **Book of Mormon** | | | |
| **Searching:** *Connections* *Patterns* *Themes* | | | |

*Insights, Experiences, Revelations*

_____
_____
_____
_____
_____
_____
_____
_____
_____
_____
_____
_____
_____
_____
_____
_____
_____
_____

WEEK OF                              TO

| Wednesday | Thursday | Friday | Saturday |
|---|---|---|---|
|  |  |  |  |
|  |  |  |  |
|  |  |  |  |

_____
_____
_____
_____
_____
_____
_____
_____
_____
_____
_____
_____
_____
_____
_____
_____

# SCRIPTURE JOURNAL

*Topics Studied:*

|  | *Sunday* | *Monday* | *Tuesday* |
|---|---|---|---|
| **Come Follow Me** | | | |
| **Book of Mormon** | | | |
| **Searching:** *Connections*  *Patterns*  *Themes* | | | |

*Insights, Experiences, Revelations*

_____
_____
_____
_____
_____
_____
_____
_____
_____
_____
_____
_____
_____
_____
_____
_____
_____
_____

WEEK OF                                    TO

| Wednesday | Thursday | Friday | Saturday |
|---|---|---|---|
|  |  |  |  |
|  |  |  |  |
|  |  |  |  |

_____
_____
_____
_____
_____
_____
_____
_____
_____
_____
_____
_____
_____
_____
_____
_____

# SCRIPTURE JOURNAL

*Topics Studied:*

|  | Sunday | Monday | Tuesday |
|---|---|---|---|
| Come Follow Me | | | |
| Book of Mormon | | | |
| Searching: *Connections* *Patterns* *Themes* | | | |

*Insights, Experiences, Revelations*

_____
_____
_____
_____
_____
_____
_____
_____
_____
_____
_____
_____
_____
_____
_____
_____
_____
_____

WEEK OF                              TO

| Wednesday | Thursday | Friday | Saturday |
|---|---|---|---|
|  |  |  |  |
|  |  |  |  |
|  |  |  |  |

# SCRIPTURE JOURNAL

*Topics Studied:*

|  | *Sunday* | *Monday* | *Tuesday* |
|---|---|---|---|
| Come Follow Me | | | |
| Book of Mormon | | | |
| Searching: *Connections*  *Patterns*  *Themes* | | | |

*Insights, Experiences, Revelations*

_____
_____
_____
_____
_____
_____
_____
_____
_____
_____
_____
_____
_____
_____
_____
_____
_____
_____

WEEK OF                              TO

| Wednesday | Thursday | Friday | Saturday |
|---|---|---|---|
| | | | |
| | | | |
| | | | |

_____
_____
_____
_____
_____
_____
_____
_____
_____
_____
_____
_____
_____
_____
_____
_____

# SCRIPTURE JOURNAL

*Topics Studied:*

|  | *Sunday* | *Monday* | *Tuesday* |
|---|---|---|---|
| **Come Follow Me** | | | |
| **Book of Mormon** | | | |
| **Searching:** *Connections* *Patterns* *Themes* | | | |

*Insights, Experiences, Revelations*

_____
_____
_____
_____
_____
_____
_____
_____
_____
_____
_____
_____
_____
_____
_____
_____
_____
_____

WEEK OF	TO

| Wednesday | Thursday | Friday | Saturday |
|---|---|---|---|
|  |  |  |  |
|  |  |  |  |
|  |  |  |  |

# SCRIPTURE JOURNAL

*Topics Studied:*

|  | *Sunday* | *Monday* | *Tuesday* |
|---|---|---|---|
| Come Follow Me |  |  |  |
| Book of Mormon |  |  |  |
| Searching: *Connections* *Patterns* *Themes* |  |  |  |

*Insights, Experiences, Revelations*

_____
_____
_____
_____
_____
_____
_____
_____
_____
_____
_____
_____
_____
_____
_____
_____
_____

WEEK OF                          TO

| Wednesday | Thursday | Friday | Saturday |
|---|---|---|---|
|  |  |  |  |
|  |  |  |  |
|  |  |  |  |

# SCRIPTURE JOURNAL

*Topics Studied:*

|  | Sunday | Monday | Tuesday |
|---|---|---|---|
| **Come Follow Me** | | | |
| **Book of Mormon** | | | |
| Searching: *Connections* *Patterns* *Themes* | | | |

*Insights, Experiences, Revelations*

_____
_____
_____
_____
_____
_____
_____
_____
_____
_____
_____
_____
_____
_____
_____
_____
_____
_____

WEEK OF                              TO

| Wednesday | Thursday | Friday | Saturday |
|---|---|---|---|
|  |  |  |  |
|  |  |  |  |
|  |  |  |  |

_____
_____
_____
_____
_____
_____
_____
_____
_____
_____
_____
_____
_____
_____
_____

# SCRIPTURE JOURNAL

*Topics Studied:*

|  | *Sunday* | *Monday* | *Tuesday* |
|---|---|---|---|
| Come Follow Me | | | |
| Book of Mormon | | | |
| Searching: *Connections* *Patterns* *Themes* | | | |

*Insights, Experiences, Revelations*

_____
_____
_____
_____
_____
_____
_____
_____
_____
_____
_____
_____
_____
_____
_____
_____
_____

WEEK OF                              TO

| Wednesday | Thursday | Friday | Saturday |
|---|---|---|---|
|  |  |  |  |
|  |  |  |  |
|  |  |  |  |

# SCRIPTURE JOURNAL

*Topics Studied:*

|  | *Sunday* | *Monday* | *Tuesday* |
|---|---|---|---|
| **Come Follow Me** | | | |
| **Book of Mormon** | | | |
| **Searching:** *Connections* *Patterns* *Themes* | | | |

*Insights, Experiences, Revelations*

_____
_____
_____
_____
_____
_____
_____
_____
_____
_____
_____
_____
_____
_____
_____
_____
_____
_____

WEEK OF                                    TO

| Wednesday | Thursday | Friday | Saturday |
|---|---|---|---|
|  |  |  |  |
|  |  |  |  |
|  |  |  |  |

# SCRIPTURE JOURNAL

*Topics Studied:*

|  | *Sunday* | *Monday* | *Tuesday* |
|---|---|---|---|
| Come Follow Me | | | |
| Book of Mormon | | | |
| Searching: *Connections* *Patterns* *Themes* | | | |

*Insights, Experiences, Revelations*

_____
_____
_____
_____
_____
_____
_____
_____
_____
_____
_____
_____
_____
_____
_____
_____

WEEK OF                              TO

| Wednesday | Thursday | Friday | Saturday |
|---|---|---|---|
|  |  |  |  |
|  |  |  |  |
|  |  |  |  |

_____
_____
_____
_____
_____
_____
_____
_____
_____
_____
_____
_____
_____
_____
_____
_____

# SCRIPTURE JOURNAL

*Topics Studied:*

|  | *Sunday* | *Monday* | *Tuesday* |
|---|---|---|---|
| **Come Follow Me** | | | |
| **Book of Mormon** | | | |
| **Searching:** *Connections* *Patterns* *Themes* | | | |

*Insights, Experiences, Revelations*

_____
_____
_____
_____
_____
_____
_____
_____
_____
_____
_____
_____
_____
_____
_____
_____
_____

WEEK OF                                        TO

| Wednesday | Thursday | Friday | Saturday |
|-----------|----------|--------|----------|
|           |          |        |          |
|           |          |        |          |
|           |          |        |          |

_____
_____
_____
_____
_____
_____
_____
_____
_____
_____
_____
_____
_____
_____
_____
_____

# SCRIPTURE JOURNAL

*Topics Studied:*

|  | Sunday | Monday | Tuesday |
|---|---|---|---|
| Come Follow Me | | | |
| Book of Mormon | | | |
| Searching: *Connections* *Patterns* *Themes* | | | |

*Insights, Experiences, Revelations*

_____
_____
_____
_____
_____
_____
_____
_____
_____
_____
_____
_____
_____
_____
_____
_____
_____
_____

WEEK OF                              TO

| Wednesday | Thursday | Friday | Saturday |
|---|---|---|---|
|  |  |  |  |
|  |  |  |  |
|  |  |  |  |

# SCRIPTURE JOURNAL

*Topics Studied:*

|  | *Sunday* | *Monday* | *Tuesday* |
|---|---|---|---|
| **Come Follow Me** | | | |
| **Book of Mormon** | | | |
| **Searching:** *Connections* *Patterns* *Themes* | | | |

*Insights, Experiences, Revelations*

_____
_____
_____
_____
_____
_____
_____
_____
_____
_____
_____
_____
_____
_____
_____
_____
_____
_____

WEEK OF                              TO

| Wednesday | Thursday | Friday | Saturday |
|-----------|----------|--------|----------|
|           |          |        |          |
|           |          |        |          |
|           |          |        |          |

_____
_____
_____
_____
_____
_____
_____
_____
_____
_____
_____
_____
_____
_____
_____
_____

# SCRIPTURE JOURNAL

*Topics Studied:*

|  | *Sunday* | *Monday* | *Tuesday* |
|---|---|---|---|
| **Come Follow Me** | | | |
| **Book of Mormon** | | | |
| **Searching:** *Connections* *Patterns* *Themes* | | | |

*Insights, Experiences, Revelations*

_____
_____
_____
_____
_____
_____
_____
_____
_____
_____
_____
_____
_____
_____
_____
_____
_____

WEEK OF                              TO

| Wednesday | Thursday | Friday | Saturday |
|-----------|----------|--------|----------|
|           |          |        |          |
|           |          |        |          |
|           |          |        |          |

_____
_____
_____
_____
_____
_____
_____
_____
_____
_____
_____
_____
_____
_____
_____
_____
_____

# SCRIPTURE JOURNAL

*Topics Studied:*

|  | Sunday | Monday | Tuesday |
|---|---|---|---|
| Come Follow Me | | | |
| Book of Mormon | | | |
| Searching: *Connections* *Patterns* *Themes* | | | |

*Insights, Experiences, Revelations*

_____
_____
_____
_____
_____
_____
_____
_____
_____
_____
_____
_____
_____
_____
_____
_____
_____

WEEK OF                              TO

| Wednesday | Thursday | Friday | Saturday |
|-----------|----------|--------|----------|
|           |          |        |          |
|           |          |        |          |
|           |          |        |          |

_____
_____
_____
_____
_____
_____
_____
_____
_____
_____
_____
_____
_____
_____
_____
_____
_____

# SCRIPTURE JOURNAL

*Topics Studied:*

|  | Sunday | Monday | Tuesday |
|---|---|---|---|
| Come Follow Me | | | |
| Book of Mormon | | | |
| Searching: *Connections* *Patterns* *Themes* | | | |

*Insights, Experiences, Revelations*

_____
_____
_____
_____
_____
_____
_____
_____
_____
_____
_____
_____
_____
_____
_____
_____
_____

WEEK OF                              TO

| Wednesday | Thursday | Friday | Saturday |
|-----------|----------|--------|----------|
|           |          |        |          |
|           |          |        |          |
|           |          |        |          |

_____
_____
_____
_____
_____
_____
_____
_____
_____
_____
_____
_____
_____
_____
_____
_____

# SCRIPTURE JOURNAL

*Topics Studied:*

|  | Sunday | Monday | Tuesday |
|---|---|---|---|
| **Come Follow Me** | | | |
| **Book of Mormon** | | | |
| Searching: *Connections*  *Patterns*  *Themes* | | | |

*Insights, Experiences, Revelations*

_____
_____
_____
_____
_____
_____
_____
_____
_____
_____
_____
_____
_____
_____
_____
_____
_____

WEEK OF TO

| Wednesday | Thursday | Friday | Saturday |
|---|---|---|---|
|  |  |  |  |
|  |  |  |  |
|  |  |  |  |

_____
_____
_____
_____
_____
_____
_____
_____
_____
_____
_____
_____
_____
_____
_____
_____

# SCRIPTURE JOURNAL

*Topics Studied:*

|  | *Sunday* | *Monday* | *Tuesday* |
|---|---|---|---|
| Come Follow Me | | | |
| Book of Mormon | | | |
| Searching: *Connections* *Patterns* *Themes* | | | |

*Insights, Experiences, Revelations*

_____
_____
_____
_____
_____
_____
_____
_____
_____
_____
_____
_____
_____
_____
_____
_____
_____

WEEK OF                                TO

| Wednesday | Thursday | Friday | Saturday |
|-----------|----------|--------|----------|
|           |          |        |          |
|           |          |        |          |
|           |          |        |          |

_____
_____
_____
_____
_____
_____
_____
_____
_____
_____
_____
_____
_____
_____
_____
_____
_____

*Preparing for General Conference*

Counsel I have applied from last Conference

_____
_____
_____
_____
_____
_____
_____
_____
_____

My Questions

_____
_____
_____
_____
_____
_____
_____
_____
_____
_____
_____

Answers Received

_____
_____
_____
_____
_____
_____
_____
_____
_____
_____
_____
_____
_____
_____
_____

# General Conference Notes

Day/Session

Music notes

_____
_____
_____
_____

Speaker

Notes & Impressions

_____
_____
_____
_____
_____
_____
_____
_____
_____
_____
_____
_____
_____
_____
_____
_____
_____
_____
_____
_____
_____
_____
_____
_____

Speaker

Notes & Impressions

_____
_____
_____
_____
_____
_____
_____
_____
_____
_____
_____
_____
_____
_____
_____
_____

Speaker

Notes & Impressions

_____
_____
_____
_____
_____
_____
_____
_____
_____
_____
_____
_____
_____
_____
_____
_____

Speaker

Notes & Impressions

Speaker

Notes & Impressions

Speaker

Notes & Impressions

_____
_____
_____
_____
_____
_____
_____
_____
_____
_____
_____
_____
_____
_____
_____
_____
_____

Speaker

Notes & Impressions

_____
_____
_____
_____
_____
_____
_____
_____
_____
_____
_____
_____
_____
_____
_____
_____
_____

# General Conference Notes

Day/Session

Music notes

---
---
---
---

Speaker

Notes & Impressions

Speaker

Notes & Impressions

Speaker

Notes & Impressions

Speaker

Notes & Impressions

Speaker

Notes & Impressions

Speaker

Notes & Impressions

_____
_____
_____
_____
_____
_____
_____
_____
_____
_____
_____
_____
_____
_____
_____
_____
_____

Speaker

Notes & Impressions

_____
_____
_____
_____
_____
_____
_____
_____
_____
_____
_____
_____
_____
_____
_____
_____
_____

# General Conference Notes

Day/Session

Music notes

___

Speaker

Notes & Impressions

Speaker

Notes & Impressions

Speaker

Notes & Impressions

Speaker

Notes & Impressions

Speaker

Notes & Impressions

Speaker

Notes & Impressions

___

Speaker

Notes & Impressions

# General Conference Notes

Day/Session

Music notes

_____
_____
_____
_____

Speaker

Notes & Impressions

_____
_____
_____
_____
_____
_____
_____
_____
_____
_____
_____
_____
_____
_____
_____
_____
_____
_____
_____
_____
_____
_____
_____
_____
_____
_____

Speaker

Notes & Impressions

_____
_____
_____
_____
_____
_____
_____
_____
_____
_____
_____
_____
_____
_____
_____
_____
_____

Speaker

Notes & Impressions

_____
_____
_____
_____
_____
_____
_____
_____
_____
_____
_____
_____
_____
_____
_____
_____
_____

Speaker

Notes & Impressions

Speaker

Notes & Impressions

Speaker

Notes & Impressions

_____
_____
_____
_____
_____
_____
_____
_____
_____
_____
_____
_____
_____
_____
_____

Speaker

Notes & Impressions

_____
_____
_____
_____
_____
_____
_____
_____
_____
_____
_____
_____
_____
_____
_____

# General Conference Notes

Day/Session

Music notes

_____
_____
_____
_____

Speaker

Notes & Impressions

_____
_____
_____
_____
_____
_____
_____
_____
_____
_____
_____
_____
_____
_____
_____
_____
_____
_____
_____
_____
_____
_____
_____
_____
_____

Speaker

Notes & Impressions

___

Speaker

Notes & Impressions

Speaker

Notes & Impressions

Speaker

Notes & Impressions

Speaker

Notes & Impressions

___

Speaker

Notes & Impressions

___

*Preparing for Conference*

Counsel I have applied from last Conference

My Questions

Answers Received

General Conference Notes

Day/Session

Music notes

Speaker

Notes & Impressions

Speaker

Notes & Impressions

Speaker

Notes & Impressions

Speaker

Notes & Impressions

Speaker

Notes & Impressions

Speaker

Notes & Impressions

Speaker

Notes & Impressions

# General Conference Notes

Day/Session

Music notes

___

Speaker

Notes & Impressions

Speaker

Notes & Impressions

Speaker

Notes & Impressions

Speaker

Notes & Impressions

_____
_____
_____
_____
_____
_____
_____
_____
_____
_____
_____
_____
_____
_____
_____

Speaker

Notes & Impressions

_____
_____
_____
_____
_____
_____
_____
_____
_____
_____
_____
_____
_____
_____
_____

Speaker

Notes & Impressions

_____
_____
_____
_____
_____
_____
_____
_____
_____
_____
_____
_____
_____
_____
_____
_____
_____

Speaker

Notes & Impressions

_____
_____
_____
_____
_____
_____
_____
_____
_____
_____
_____
_____
_____
_____
_____
_____
_____

# General Conference Notes

Day/Session

Music notes

_____
_____
_____
_____

Speaker

Notes & Impressions

_____
_____
_____
_____
_____
_____
_____
_____
_____
_____
_____
_____
_____
_____
_____
_____
_____
_____
_____
_____
_____
_____
_____
_____

Speaker

Notes & Impressions

Speaker

Notes & Impressions

Speaker

Notes & Impressions

_____
_____
_____
_____
_____
_____
_____
_____
_____
_____
_____
_____
_____
_____
_____
_____
_____

Speaker

Notes & Impressions

_____
_____
_____
_____
_____
_____
_____
_____
_____
_____
_____
_____
_____
_____
_____
_____
_____

Speaker

Notes & Impressions

Speaker

Notes & Impressions

# General Conference Notes

Day/Session

Music notes

___

Speaker

Notes & Impressions

Speaker

Notes & Impressions

_____
_____
_____
_____
_____
_____
_____
_____
_____
_____
_____
_____
_____
_____
_____
_____
_____
_____

Speaker

Notes & Impressions

_____
_____
_____
_____
_____
_____
_____
_____
_____
_____
_____
_____
_____
_____
_____
_____
_____
_____

Speaker

Notes & Impressions

_____
_____
_____
_____
_____
_____
_____
_____
_____
_____
_____
_____
_____
_____
_____
_____

Speaker

Notes & Impressions

_____
_____
_____
_____
_____
_____
_____
_____
_____
_____
_____
_____
_____
_____
_____
_____

Speaker

Notes & Impressions

Speaker

Notes & Impressions

# The year in review

How have I changed?

___

What questions do I have for the coming year's study?

___

www.ingramcontent.com/pod-product-compliance
Lightning Source LLC
Chambersburg PA
CBHW081748100526
44592CB00015B/2344